QUEST FOR GOD
QUEST FOR SELF

QUEST FOR GOD
QUEST FOR SELF

meditations on religion and self-awareness

LOUIS CHRISTIAENS S.J.

Fides/Claretian
Notre Dame, Indiana 46556

Translated from the French by Marie-Odile Fortier-Masek

Photographic sources

Vernon Sigl: *pages 3, 11, 20, 29, 45, 54, 63, 70, 84*

Ron Parent: *page 37*

Mary Ellen Kronstein: *page 77*

Imprimi potest: Daniel L. Flaherty, S.J.
Provincial, Chicago Province

Nihil obstat: Terry E. Place
Censor librorum

Imprimatur: †William E. McManus
Bishop of Fort Wayne-South Bend

© 1979, Fides/Claretian
Notre Dame, Indiana 46556

Library of Congress Cataloging in Publication Data

Christiaens, Louis, 1935–
  Quest for God, quest for self.

  Collection of excerpts of meditations previously
published in France.
  1. Meditations. I. Title.
BX2182.2.C53 1979   242   79-4687
ISBN 0-8190-0631-9

I

Introduction

"The rose doesn't ask the why of things,
It comes to flower as it always does.
It is not anxious for its own concern,
It doesn't even wonder if it can be seen."

Angelus Silesius

PILGRIM of life, to you this book. The friend you chose to take along. An open word, whispered to you. A word for you to welcome, unique, fragile, never final. A word offered to you, for you alone to hear, to keep. A word to help you on your way. Don't expect miracles from the words you read. You see them, you meet them. In the night of your fears and doubts, they might enkindle a new light. In the desert of your solitude, they might bring to bloom the flower of gratitude. Strange power of words. . . . Words that can destroy or build, hurt or soothe, kill or give life.

Indeed, you feel strong. You feel that you can bear anything, as long as there is a friend near you. Especially if that friend is silent. This book wants to be your friend. Through its pages you might find a new flavor to live, a desire to exist for those around you. It dares to take you to the foot of that cliff which defies climbing, yet fascinates you: God, the Absolute. Your God . . . Hazy mystery, who calls you to live, to love.

These texts have already helped a few of your companions on their journey of life. They have pondered about the same questions which haunt your mind, stumbled over the same answers: "Where are we going? Why do we even go? Is it a long walk? For whom do we live?" Some of the words they gleaned along the pages have fallen into fertile ground, changing their whole lives.

Through the rhythmic pulsation of those pages they have let go of their occidental impatience, that haste which pushes civilized people toward challenges forgotten as soon as they are met, so preoccupied are they by new goals. They have rediscovered that to be called civilized, man has to be free. Free to love his fellow men, free to love his God.

In the United States as well as in France, the same words in their fragile strength, have brought light and life. It's that simple. The poor cry out, God listens, God sends us his Son, the Living Word.

Let these words lead you. Let their power work in you. Words are a bond between your daily life and your inner life. What you read, what you enjoy will become a part of you. If you made this book yours, isn't it because you already bear it—in you before you have even read it? A new birth takes place, in the depth of the being, in him who gives us growth for eternal life.

Don't ask yourself any questions about the author of that book or those who participated in it. In their own way they have been called to progress on the same road as yours, in quest of themselves, in quest of others, in quest of God. They feel a deep detachment toward what they are giving to you. In fact, nothing comes from them. They have received everything. They are aware of their own poverty, of their fragility. Yet, they have hope, source of their joy in front of the wonders of a God who gives and forgives, and gathers in his love a body of people truly alive.

Lay yourself open to the promptings of these texts, which draw you into the center of your longings. Gradually you will become what you read, what you are, closer to a full humanity and to your God.

GOD

Wind of Love

PRAYER is the opposite of anemia. It is the anemone,
which, in Greek, means breeze. The wind. . . . Prayer is
that tiny little flower, swept by the mighty wind of love. A
little flower so light that it becomes breeze. So light that it
becomes the other. To pray is to become the other. To
become the breeze. To be raptured by the spirit. The wind
blows wherever it wills. No one knows from where it comes
or where it goes. Prayer is the breath of the soul, impossible
to capture. Prayer longs for love. Love inspires prayer. Love
is free. Prayer sings that feeling of gratuity. It is not made
for any special purpose. It is. It is man's meaningful smile to
God.

Prayer is act of love. Prayer is act of faith. Love, faith
are the wagers. At stake is man's destiny. The world's destiny. The church's destiny. If prayer would disappear from
the surface of the earth, what would become of man left
without his inferiority, of the world left without its motiva-
tion, of the church left without communion?

To Pray Is Impossible

TO PRAY is impossible. Whoever pretends to be able to pray
is somehow claiming to have the power of making God
appear. Most strange magic! He merely unleashes his phan-
tasms, his fears, maybe the mother of his dreams, his terrify-
ing tyrant, the mirror of his psyche.

We should start by recognizing that prayer itself is

impossible. Prayer as such, not as a statement, not as statements to God, but as the very act of praying. It begins with a non-prayer prayer, a deep silence without God, in which any pious word is lost. There, man is stark naked, like at birth. Could he still be given a chance to be born to what, by his obstinacy and his fears, he keeps on missing by pretending to grasp? Don't ask me what it is: Who would even know? It might be that open space in which each human being has the right and the strength to exist? or, is it, quite simply, to be? To be and to wait.

What we might have lived and felt, as man, as woman: our anger, anxieties, needs, distress, even depression is finally accepted.

Prayer requires total trust and humility. We must see life as a gift, realize that it is good and that we have to live it. After that, anything goes! Rites or non-rites; the repetition of some sacred links of words, or the word which comes up and falls at random, the revered icon or the absence of image, the dialogue or the solitude, the thought rising toward the unreachable or the familiar invocation. The bountiful array of speeches, songs, architecture, or the barren emptiness, the big empty space without a face or even a voice except for the most pure, most silent voice. The voice which speaks before the world comes into being.

Freedom! A place for human communication, surrounded by nothing, preceded by nothing. Would there be such a place where we could love anybody like our neighbor?

Patience. . . . Silence

PRAYER tends toward silence. A well-filled silence. A silence close to the silence which follows music. The song has waned . . . yet, for a long time, its presence lingers, demanding total silence and quiet.

To pray, to progress in prayer, to advance in our union with God is, oddly enough, to become acquainted with an ever more complete poverty. It is to stammer endlessly and blissfully, through the naive rudiments of pure faith.

In front of God, such as he is, I stand, such as I am, incredibly indigent, in need of everything, stuttering. Yes, here I am, in front of him, the most beautiful, the holy, the unique in everything. Love in its fullness and majesty.

And who will ever say how much prayer is patience? Yes, more and more patience? An endless patience to bear the silence, to bear the night, to bear the grueling wanderings of the mind until it please God's love to come down again and suddenly to fill our soul up to the brim.

Prayer and patience.
  Prayer and waiting.
    Prayer of simple attention.
      Prayer of total submission.
        Abandonment to the Father.
Prayer and faith.
  Prayer that is faith itself.
    Silent,
    ardent
    adoration of the faith.

At Night They Stood

AT NIGHT they stood, vigilant. Erect, under the stars, straight as trees, their hands raised to the sky, they were turned toward that spot in the horizon, where the morning sun would rise.

All night, their bodies in longing desire would be awaiting for the day to break. It was their prayer. They had no words. And why words?... Their words were their bodies, in the labor of waiting. That labor of gnawing desire was their silent prayer.

They were there, that's all.

At morn, when the first rays of the sun would brush the palm of their hands, they would know that time had come to rest.

For the sun had arrived.

Silence and Word

SILENCE belongs to the most impressive events of our life. One day, we are told, Saint Dominic came to visit Saint Francis of Assisi. They embraced. Not a word. They parted. Not a word. A moving scene. God reveals himself to us in silence, through silence. Yet it is hard, in our daily lives, to bear the silence of God. We are afraid of it.

From silence are born the most beautiful words of man. Silence is the enkindled furnace of speech. Silence is the melting pot of words and essential impressions or essential thoughts. Any creative impulse is also born from silence, from a long, abiding peace. When music reaches its true beauty, it comes to an end. At such instants we foresee a mystery, which we want to keep from mingling with wordly things. That is why we make silence.

What is impossible to understand, though, is that God, the absolute mystery, can speak to us. How? Our God of Silence speaks to us through his prophet Hosea. He says: "I shall lead you to the desert and then I shall speak to you." The men to whom God speaks and through whom he speaks to us, are always those whom he has led to the desert, solitude of pain, of inner hunger, of gasping desire, and who became totally silent. From a silence deeply intertwined with pain and desire are born the words we use in talking. Words snatched from the depths of the mystery by some blood-stained hands. Words which can never be forgotten from the instant we hear them. As in the beatitudes, we can understand them immediately, in an immediate perception. We can make them part of ourselves and still we can never totally grasp their meaning. They are too profound for us and, yet, we understand them. We understand why Christ proclaims the little ones, the humble ones, as truly blessed, for they already possess an authentic happiness. Essential words are always inner events. Events born out of love. When he said, "My sheep recognize my voice," Christ was thinking of the humble ones.

———···✦···———

As I Listen to You

FAITH is welcome.

To welcome we have to learn how to wait, vigilant as a watchman who wants to be fully aware, vulnerable as we might be, surprised or even seduced. Such a watch requires the undivided attention of our heart and senses. Our eye, so sharp when we want to focus on target, becomes blind, dazzled by the unexpected lightning. That is why we need our ear, our ear so fine that it can perceive the least sign of an approach, but also the ear we turn to answer the unexpected presence. Our faith is like an obedient ear.

The obedience of faith is first of all a way to listen. In many languages the same word is used for obedience and for listening. Obedience must not be blind, obedience cannot be deaf. If we wish to establish a dialogue we have to let the other person fashion our ear. Yet, there is an Other one who has been talking since the beginning, who has fashioned my ear so that I can listen to him and here I am, willing to plug my ears so that I do not have to listen to him. Yes, when someone talks to me he is asking me for one thing: would I please listen to him! But I am afraid of the answer I might have to give to him. Whether I run away or whether I withdraw from it, I want to avoid the word which is after me. Would it be because of the image I have of the request? I do not want to be deprived of what I have. I am afraid that some despot might decide my fate.

To refuse to listen is to refuse to obey. But which obedience is requested from me? Which demand is made to me?

Faith has enabled us to listen by revealing that the Other does not even want to ask, he wants to give. He is not trying to dominate us, but to set a dialogue with us.

Yes, I Do Know You!

OH! my child, you have not known who you are. You don't even know yourself yet. I mean that you have not known yourself yet as the object of my love. Furthermore, you have not known what you are in me and all the potential that rests in you.

Arouse from that sleep, from those bad dreams! In some rare moments of truth, you see in yourself only failures, defeats, downfalls, impurities, maybe crimes too. But all those are not you. Not your real self. Not your deep-down self.

Under and beyond all those, under and beyond sin, transgressions, failures, I do see you.

I see you and I love you. I do love your real self. It is not the evil you did, though it cannot be ignored, denied or even lessened—can black be white—but it is beyond it, much deeper, that I see something still alive.

Those masks you put on, that disguise you wear may hide you from the eyes of others or even from your own self but not from me, for I pursue you like no one has ever pursued you.

That look, your look no longer clear, your feverish, gasping desire for what seems so intense to you, those precarious spasms, the harshness and pettiness of your heart, all those I set apart from you. I sever all that from you, I throw it far away.

Listen! No one truly understands you, yet, I do. I could tell you so many great and beautiful things about yourself. Yes, so many I could tell. . . . Not of that self of yours that the power of darkness has lured so often, but of you, the one whom I wished into being. You are the one who rests in me as a thought, as an intention to love. Yes, you are the one who could still visibly be.

Become visibly what you are in my thought. Be the ultimate reality of your own self. Enkindle those powers I have placed in you.

For in just about any man or woman there is the same potential of inner beauty and goodness that there is in you. There is no divine gift for which you could not hope, those you will receive as a whole if you love with me and in me.

Whatever you might have done in your past, those bonds I break, and, if I break them, who shall prevent you from getting up and walking?

Let There Be Light

SIX TIMES in the first chapter of Genesis God is shown creating the days of the week and setting evening as the starting point of the day.

O Lord, how different is the way men of today count time! Almost instinctively men perceive morning as the beginning of their day.

The day starts with the first light of daybreak. Then comes the joy of dawn, the rise of the sun, the glory of midday, dusk, twilight, the sadness of nightfall and, finally, the day's tragic collapse and the terror of darkness.

For you, Lord, it is not so. You tell us that first there was evening and then came morning.

Your day starts in the evening, in the darkness of night. It unfolds toward the morning, toward the light, toward the blaze of the burning bush, toward the midday sun.

And so it is with our love: forever budding, forever fragile, uncertain and insecure. It will blossom toward the radiance of boundless love.

No doubt night will return, yet there is a world of difference between the perception of a day which sinks into the night and a day which rises up to the morning.

What is important, Lord, is the sense you give to the movement of the day. Out of this order you create a symbol for us. Since the beginning you have oriented the evolution of time toward your resplendent plenitude. You orient us toward morning.

Lord, let me better understand the becoming and the bearing of my days. In spite of the obscurity of the moment, grant me the intuition of the rising of the sun of Love. Open wide my hope to the call of the forthcoming day of your kingdom, which does not know the night.

Quest of God

IF YOU WISH to choose the road of contemplation in your search for God, do not see your quest as illusive. God is awaiting. . . .

Your very desire to search for him comes from him. It is his call to you. He might not want you to know it, but, believe me, that desire comes from him. He has set in you the desire to search for him. Of his own hands, he has prepared provisions for your journey. He has even planned your stopovers.

Whether he shows himself or not, it does not matter.

With loving care he has planned shelter, meals on your road. Maybe somewhere will you recognize him at the breaking of the bread. Maybe he will walk along with you for a short distance.

In this world no one can see God without dying, yet only those who will see him will live. That is true. We cannot see God, yet God shows himself to us. Some have looked for him before you and have found him. It was not because of their efforts, yet, without any effort they would not have succeeded either.

That desire you have to find God, that desire which springs from your deep down self, that desire which is your own, not your neighbor's, that very desire is, at its roots, a desire which comes from God.

A desire which carries you to your God.

And your God lovingly awaits for the desire he has set in you to become totally a part of your whole being before he gives himself to you. You do not chase him, you do not grasp him, you do not force him to give himself to you. He makes you feel his presence, he shows and reveals himself to you. . . .

You are set to go on your search for God, still you do not know under which face he will show himself to you. Perhaps he will remain faceless, nameless. You will be short of words to define him when you see him. . . . So, leave, filled with an immense desire, but forget names, representations, definitions, visions. . . . For God is God. He is way beyond what we can say or think, beyond all that we can even see of him. We call him God, but, as a matter of fact, he has no name. When Moses asked him for his name, remember, he did not give him any name, he simply answered: "I am."

Yes, he is, and you too, are.

You are from him, by him.

It is through that bond of your whole being that you will catch a glimpse of him. . . . Far beyond concepts and words, but in our self, through the gift of his own self to you.

You dream of dazzling light, maybe you will have to walk through night and deserts. You dream of shimmering lights and yet you will walk through darkness. . . . But in that darkness, there is God.

And he is your God.

--------··◦◦••--------

When You Hide. . . .

LORD, I pray to you tonight, as I feel better, for that day, may be soon to come, when I am again exhausted and in pain. That day when the biggest temptation would be not to pray. Humbly I beg you to grant me then your help and your grace and strength to be in union with the prayer of your son in Gethsemani, during his agony. For the greater the pain, the greater our need to pray. Keep away from me the thought that prayer is impossible at those hours of suffering.

Through the gospel, you show me prayer as a vital act. Like breathing. Isn't it also the glance of the child toward a Father who is in heavens, the acceptance of our misery or the naive supplication to the one from whom all good things come?

Prayer: quiet conversation . . . heart-to-heart chat. . . .

Yet, in danger, in dire pain, prayer: the scream, the plea, the writhing supplication of our whole self.

Like that young child I saw in the street, who thought he was lost and cried desperately "Daddy, Daddy!" He could not have cared less about what passers-by might think or say. Hiccups and sobs left him breathless. He is frantic, and, then, suddenly, he is grabbed, lifted off the ground by two hefty arms. He is squeezed tight against a chest quite familiar to him. And here he is, with his Dad, laughing wholeheartedly of his fright. . . .

My prayer? Precisely that, Lord: to try to find you . . . when you hide!

A Farewell to Ourselves

ONCE we are set to go and search for God, we must pack, saddle our mount, and get on our way. On the horizon stands God's mountain, barely visible. At dawn we must leave.

It is no small venture. We must bid farewell. A farewell to what? To everything and to nothing. A farewell to nothing, for this world we leave will be here forever: it will stay next to us, within us, until our last breath, as close to us as ever. By trying to drive it out of ourselves, to reject it, we give it more chances of making a vehement comeback inside ourselves. A farewell to everything, since by leaving for our search for the absolute, we burn bridges from whatever would interfere with our goal and also with whatever in us or in others could foster opposition to the divine action. Finally, and by far the hardest to leave behind is that self of ours which, by its intrinsic need for autonomy, makes opposition to God.

Thus, separation is not distance but rather detachment. First we have to prevent our personality from withdrawing, from creating a citadel between God and ourselves, in which he would be admitted only as a guest.

Yes, when you want to pray, open your house, let your soul open out in front of God.

Every kind of life requires a kind of detachment. Let the soul of the spouses or of the engaged couple detach from itself, open out, for, without detachment no love is possible. It is just an egotistic search of one self through the other.

The climax of love is God's love, a love which is a total and reciprocal gift of one to the other. For us, men, God is the other, that other who finally will reveal himself through love, as the being of our being.

What should we take along on our journey? Our whole self and nothing else. It sounds like a strange answer since we said earlier that one must leave everything behind and mostly leave his own self! Still it is true, we must take along our whole self. Many of us leave only in appearance. They take along a ghost of themselves, an abstract mock-up. They protect themselves before they set out for the road. They make up an artifical personality, are borrowed from books and send that artificial self, call it robot, a shadow to search for God. Never do they let their whole self be involved in such a venture. Thus it is already a kind of saint who is sent out on that expedition, a person modeled after treatises about perfection. They send out a double of themselves to attempt that journey and nevertheless wonder why they got only disappointment out of it!

When we are ready to leave, we must load our mount

with our belongings, take along everything we are, our worthless carcass, our mind, our soul, yes, everything; our strong points and our weaknesses, our past sins, our big hopes, our vilest or most violent tendencies... everything, absolutely everything. For all must go through the fire. In the end all has to be integrated in order to make a human being able to enter body and soul into the knowledge of God.

... Once a decision to leave has been taken, once we are totally present for the departure, we must attune our body and soul perfectly to the huge body of Christ, I mean the church, we must live with it, feel the gigantic pulsations of its liturgical life, through its teachings, the sacraments, and its everlasting concern for us. Then, living in harmony with the church, it becomes easy to turn our whole being toward the Lord, and to live with the hope that soon we shall feel the weight of God's hand upon our soul.

———————— ·⦁⦀⦁· ————————

Oh, Tell Me...

Oh, tell me, who is he who listens to me,
    or with my breath does speak?
He who looks at me,
    with those eyes of mine?
He whose life is my life?

You, but you, my Lord,
    for my soul, you are. . . .
Present you are,
    and I find you.

No longer rest for me,
    to my voice, no hush.
Guide me, O Lord,
    the path of your dwelling show me.

To you I pray,
    a prayer still not a prayer, my Lord,
For my soul sees you not
    face to face.

So,
  hush,
    silence. . . .
May silence my prayer be, my Lord,
    for present are you.

———•❈•———

Blessed Be The Poor

BLESSED be the poor!

To be poor? Not too interesting. All the poor will agree!

What is interesting however is to possess the heavenly kingdom. And only the poor possess it.

Don't think that our joy should be to spend our days emptying our hands, our heads, our hearts.

Our joy is to spend our days making
a cozy little space in our hands,
    in our heads,
    in our hearts,
for the heavenly kingdom which passes by us.

Isn't it incredible to feel it so close, to know that God is near us. Isn't it fantastic also to feel that his love is possible and surrounds us,
    yet, we don't open that door,
    so unique, so simple,
        of the poverty of spirit.

Tell me why you are so sad, all of you whom God has made poor?

Don't you have any bit of hope left that you cry like those who never had any?

Let them cry those who do not know the heavy and warm presence of the kingdom of God hovering above them?

And you who know it to be at hand,
    when your riches go, at God's will,
    don't talk of poverty, but rather talk of wealth.

Become like the blindman back to his native land:
breathe the air of the kingdom, warm to its invisible sun, feel its firm ground under your feet!

Don't say: "I have lost everything," rather say: "I have gained everything."

Don't say: "Everything has been taken away from me." rather say: "I have received everything."

On your journey to meet him, leave without preconceived ideas, without that contrived weariness, without any set opinions about God, without any memories of him,

without enthusiasm,

without a whole library!

Leave without a map, for you know that he is somewhere on the road and not just at the end.

Don't try to find him through some exotic recipes,

let him find you,

in the poverty of a simple life.

Monotony is poverty, accept it.

Don't look for beautiful imaginary journeys, just be happy with the variety of kingdom of God has to offer, let it be a joy to you.

Don't be overly concerned with your life, for it is a luxury to care too much for it; for then, to you, old age will sing of birth, death of resurrection.

Time will appear like a small fold in the vast eternity. You will judge all things according to their little impact on the scale of eternity.

If you truly love the kingdom of heaven, you will rejoice to feel your intelligence at a loss in front of the divine realities and you will strive to become a better believer.

If your prayer lacks tender emotions, you will have to learn that you do not reach God with your plain nerves.

If you lack courage, still rejoice for you have the privilege to hope.

If you find others boring, if your heart feels miserable, rejoice for you carry within you that imperceptible charity!

The Treasure and The Pearl

THE PARABLES of the treasure and the pearl reveal one of the deepest exigencies of the kingdom. The kingdom is not something that could just be superimposed over our personal life, even if we would devote to it a large share of our thought and activities. One is truly concerned about the kingdom only if this concern prevails over everything else. The kingdom is absolute: it does not tolerate an off-and-on feeling. It is not something that you half-possess or to which you give only a "fair" share. You possess it only when you have given up everything else for it. The one who has found the treasure goes and sells all his belongings. The one who wants to acquire the unique pearl goes and sells all his belongings. In other words, Christian life lived in its integrity ignores sharing. It becomes real only when it takes everything away. This is what makes it different from all other ways of life. Intellectual life, aesthetic life, social life, require that a proper balance be established. It is not so with religious life. It does not include other ways of life, but, rather, it belongs to another order. It cannot be put on the same level. By taking hold of our whole self, religious life must penetrate through our other ways of life. An authentic religious life exists only where it can invade everything. When everything has been invaded, perfection is reached. We know that on this earth perfection can never be reached. Let us still rejoice even for the smallest step accomplished toward that goal. Yet, in that direction and basic orientation, let us be aware that there is no possible compromise.

There is an exclusivism which is of God—unrelated to our human selections. God is not a created reality, rejecting all other created realities. The presence of God does not reject the human side of our selves; it penetrates it and it transforms it. As humans, we must let ourselves be totally penetrated by the presence of God if we want to be taken away from our own selves. The presence of God, in its exclusive exigency, is in harmony with a part of creation untainted by sin. Its only requirement is to renew everything. For when the spirit of God comes, it renews everything. We possess God only when God penetrates our total self, and when we accept not to possess anything else anymore. To possess God, to enter the kingdom, we must therefore give up all the other things as such; for that pearl, for that treasure, we must sell all belongings. That seems quite easy to do, but it becomes harder when superior forms of life are involved—intellectual or aesthetic life. Thus we raise the question of humanism: can God be found without man giving up his own entity? Human riches when not penetrated by God, almost always exclude him. The best becomes the worst. We end up professing to live an exclusive humanism. The indefinite enjoyment of human riches makes us miss the opportunity of acquiring the unique pearl. We worship man, not God.

The kingdom can be obtained only if we give up everything else.

A Time to Be Silent Again

SILENCE does not come from the outside. It is where we are. At the bottom of the holes we drill while searching for God, before we believe that we can meet him, we can be sure that we meet silence. Two expressions relate to silence: to be silent and to make silence. To be silent means that we have succeeded, to make silence means that we are working at it.

That is why if we would wait for silence before we pray, we might seldom pray, or if we should pray, it would not be in the part of the world most in need of prayer, in those big cities where work and pleasure plot against silence.

Silence does not exist in order to prevent us from talking. If so, it would be like dumbness, which has never been anything else than a handicap found in beings to whom God has granted speech.

To make silence is to listen to God. It is to suppress whatever would prevent us from listening to him or from hearing him. To make silence is to listen to God, wherever he speaks: to those through whom he speaks in the church and to those with whom Christ has identified himself in some other way and who are asking for some light, for our heart or even for some bread.

It is to listen to God wherever he pleases to express his will, in prayer or in some way other than prayer itself.

We need silence to fulfill God's will. We need silence. Silence extended by recollection, that other dimension of ourselves, which we maim so often, or which we even despise out of sheer ignorance. We must "collect" the traces, hints, invitations, orders of God's will, as the farmer collects his crop in the barn, as the scientist collects the fruit of his experiment. To collect ourselves—to collect—cannot be done without silence. Neither can it be done without a motion, the consequent motion. The farmer will store the harvest in the barn or he will sell it; the scientist will improve the fruit of his experiment through another experiment.

It seems impossible for me to think of a life in the spirit of the gospel and not to acknowledge that it has to be life of silence.

Let us pick out of the gospel all that Jesus has said about the "word" of God, all that he has said about "welcoming" it, "keeping" it, "making" it, "announcing" it, and soon we shall have the certainty that the good news, in order to be "known," "lived," "communicated," must be "welcomed," "collected," born in the depths of ourselves.

To deliberately commit our whole life to the gospel of Jesus Christ, to choose his words as guides along our path of life, will only be possible if our life itself makes silence.

———————

My Prayer

I OPEN my eyes to search for the light of my God, and I don't find it.

I am in the dark and though my eyes are wide open, I shall find only darkness.

What good does it do to me open my eyes in the darkness, better to open my mouth.

So, first, my mouth I shall open, asking my God to dissipate the darkness and once my God has chased the darkness away, shall I be able to open my eyes and see the light of my God.

I put my heart in the heart of my God and I said to him: "Take care of my heart, now." For I was sad all night. Tears were flowing from my eyes and I couldn't stop them.

So I told myself: "It is because I don't talk to my God that I am sad."

I got up, grabbed my catechism, and in my catechism I read about the fidelity of my God.

I was not sad any more, my tears dried and I said: Forever I shall live with my God.

One evening when the tiger was outside roaming around our village and no one would dare venture and herd the buffaloes back home. I was scared too, but I said to myself I have no right to be afraid since my God is with me.

Then I went out, for my God is with me.

God's Tenderness

"I, Yahweh, have called you. I led you by the hand. I formed you. I chose you as a covenant of the people, as a light to the nations." *Isaiah 42:6*

"Because you are precious in my eyes and special and because I love you." *Isaiah 43:4*

"I took them in my arms, yet they did not understand that I cared for them. I drew them with tender cords, with

bonds of love. I fostered them like one who raises an infant to his cheek and leans toward him." *Hosea 11:3–4.*

"He who abides in love, abides in God and God in him." *1 John 4:16*

"As a mother feeds her children and takes care of them, so was the tender love that we wished to share with you not only through the gospel of God, but also with our own souls, because you had become most dear to us." *1 Thess 2:7*

"As a father towards his children, you know that we exhorted you, encouraged you and begged you to live worthily of God who calls you unto his kingdom and glory." *1 Thess 2:11–12*

"I remember the days of yore,
I meditate on all your doings,
the work of your hands I ponder.
I stretch my hands to you;
my soul thirsts for you like parched land."
Psalm 143:5–6.

"At dawn let me hear of your love, for in you I trust. Show me the path in which I should walk. For to you I lift up my soul." *Psalm 143:8*

What Does Keep Me Alive?

What does sing in my heart?
The things of this world,
The voices of men,
The word of my God.

Bread and stones,
Sun in the water,
Trees and living creatures
Speak to me.

Men—their dreams,
Hope in their eyes,
Their yes, their no,
That is my food.

The word of my God,
His silences, how far he is:
A name. The hope
To understand the signs.

What does keep me alive?
The bread of this world,
The word of men,
The fidelity of my God.

Lord, I Love You!

Lord,
I love you.
Yet,
I don't even know
Who you are.
I love you
and one cannot call you
without loving.

Lord,
I love you,
and I don't know too well what I say
and I don't know too well how I live
but I say that I live
and that to live
means I love you.

Lord,
I love you
and it is true that I do not know how to love.
In my poverty to love
I love you even more.

Lord,
I love you.
You give me to love
like no one has ever loved
you give me to love the other
like you always have loved him.

I Shall Walk Upon The Sea

To walk upon the sea!
Don't know what possessed me.
That's me: at times racing full blast,
Only to think afterwards.
Well, sometimes,
It might be best
Not to think at all.

In the skiff were we,
    scared!
At night it was,
A stormy night.
Then, suddenly,
In the moonlight:
    His shadow.

"Never fear! It's me!
—Well, if it's you,
Won't you tell me
To come to you?
—Come here!"
I don't hesitate,
I jump over the freeboard.
Guess what!
Yes, I did walk,
And it went alright,
I should say!

Yet, listen to this:
I started to think.
But, there are times
One shouldn't think

But live,
And that's all!
When I realized where I was,
At night,
A stormy night,
I stumbled, yes,
So scared was I!
No, that's just impossible,
Don't you understand!
No one walks upon the sea.
Especially at night,
A stormy night.
So, I started to sink.

To walk upon the sea?
A little far out...
Crazy...
Not the proper thing to do...
Utterly shocking!
O.K. Get it?
But when, in fact, you walk upon the sea,
It is no time for rationalizations,
No time to get wrapped up into considerations.
That's the way you sink, my friend,
Deep into your rationalizations,
Deep into your considerations,
And, boy, do I know about it!

Not that one should not think,
But there are times,
When there is no time for thinking,
For it should have been done beforehand,
And there is a time
When all those smoky rationalizations

Will be enkindled into love's fire.
And when it catches,
Love is like fire.
It is no time to smother it
Even with pails of foamy words.

Anyhow,
For me,
Now,
It's all over.
Since I have walked upon the sea,
It's clear to me
That every time
He calls me,
I shall jump over the freeboard,
Without even thinking.

May all the wise ones
Get lost into their considerations,
If that's their fun.
As for myself
I shall walk upon the sea
And then,
If I have some time to spare,
I shall think, yes.

But only
After I've made it ashore!

YOU

About Human Life

NATURE offers nothing more beautiful than the sea. Perhaps because it has no end and unfurls the ensnaring and noble beauty of a treasure hidden in its breast. Yet, there is a sight of which I shall never get tired, which fills me with awe, it is the human being.

Is there anything more beautiful than human life? Anything more awesome? Man who can tend roses, who expresses himself through poetry, who composes music, that very same man can also build arms, decree the death of others, oppress his peers. What a long way to go before we find again and restore the unity described in the first book of Genesis! Right now, we look like a patchwork of contradictions. It might be that we keep on fooling ourselves.

One of the most important moments of my existence seems to have been the discovery of its social dimension. Only then did I become aware of its personal dimension too. Before, I had been living in the illusion of the law of the jungle, letting competition take precedence over cooperation. Therefore, I had to cast away my own desires, in order to make room for some choices which became necessary. Soon I discovered that choice calls for renunciation. We can dally with the choices life offers to us, without committing ourselves to a definite one, yet, at a crossroad, by choosing a direction we have to forgo the other ones. Sometimes we are tempted to turn back, and to take another path which looks easier but is, in fact, more sinuous. We must be patient, walk with steadfast and secure steps in the direction we chose.

Smile

Smile,
    boundless space . . .
Hard to confine.
Smile,
    beyond to words . . .
open door to a mystery.
Silence of smile,
    light of smile,
  from behind the cloud.
Smile,
  which reveals,
    oh! so little, the secret
every face hides,
  still forever unknown . . .
A way,
  vanishing at lips outline.
Bursts of a tear.

Yes, Do We Look Sunny?

MEDITATING upon beauty can be an invigorating experience, if we realize that outer beauty is nothing compared to the inner one. The first one is fugitive, it withers until death puts an end to it. the other one will not pass away, for it is of eternity. One is nature's gift to us, the other is a gift from heaven. The outer beauty of a face, of a body can be a delightful sight. To deprive ourselves of such pleasure under pretense of detachment, does not sound right to me. What matters is to admire it without making it our own. The desire to possess would spoil everything. Inner beauty does not bind the one who contemplates it. It merely captures a reflection and is perceived like the call of a presence unseen yet evident.

The more delicate our soul becomes, the more sensitive will it be to the work of grace. Quick to notice it, it grasps its beauty. Life among mediocre people can be compared to a hospital stay: not too cheerful! A universe scaled down to patients and labs. Conversation with intelligent individuals generates a joy of extraordinary quality. Intelligence stimulates the mind, lifts up the spirit. Intelligence is a source of happiness. Furthermore, meeting people endowed with inner beauty is like food from heaven on our road. Inner beauty awakens the sleepy heart. It makes it aware of a cosmic dimension in an ecstatic way. It gives birth in the shadow of mystery. Inner beauty throws its seeds around, unaware of where will fall those seeds which will never know death. After emptiness has plowed our soul, its furrows lie open, fully receptive to those seeds of beauty that will germinate in its breast.

A river crosses the garden of the house where I spend my vacation. At the end of the summer it turns to a strange color, a blend of green and gold. As a farmer explained it to me: "It is the pollen of the flowers which makes it look sunny," he said. I have remembered those words. Yes, they could be applied to those who love beauty, for they too, look "sunny."

···⌒∞⌒···

Is It Ever Too Late?

AT THE ROOT of each of our actions, we find our ego. I do not mean that coarser form of human selfishness willing to destroy the other's life in exchange for some personal advantages or eager to triumph over the other for the mere pleasure of victory. By ego I mean rather an introspective feeling, most difficult to describe, which entwines around our life and invades it. Only at some truly exceptional moment, can we go beyond that existential introspection. At a few special moments we might feel so overwhelmed with friendliness and joy that we could become really present to the others. Most of the time, we are our own slaves, even in actions which would seem entirely disinterested from an outsider's perspective. A subtle narcissism chains us down. How poignant to see how those men who strove toward the purest form of authenticity, the saints I mean, let an everlasting fight against their ego, deep-rooted in their own selves and were always defeated. By trying unconsciously to affirm our ego, every day we crush those who stand in our way.

Those little tensions, those virtuous indignations, that pretense to know better than anybody, those petty humiliations which we inflict upon our neighbor, are a cover-up for our ego. Deep beyond that attitude is buried a strange inadequacy of man to love. In our hearts we keep on betraying those whom we hold dearest. Man knows, for sure, some moments of greatness, lived with intensity, filled with supernatural, when he experiences the highs which come with the true gift of self. He might not do anything else in his whole life than to take back what he has given away in an instant of spiritual bravado and also of love. Yes, man needs an incredible amount of energy, a ferocious tenacity in his exhausting ascent through the boulders to climb up the slope of his inability to love, if he wants to have the slightest idea of the gift that is exacted from him. For man is unable to really love. At the end he is left with nothing; neither happiness nor unhappiness.

Our life is a strange and painful discrepancy between those we wished to love and our love itself. We are men, vulnerable men, thrown into the adventure of love. Each attempt to love is a heartbreaking experience. Time is too short. It is always too late for us to grasp the presence of the true gift; the opportunity has fled away. Yes, somehow, is it not always too late in our life? Too late to notice the distress of our neighbors? Too late to understand that a chance for friendship was extended to us?

Too late to recognize that someone loved us?

Love

LOVE begins when we prefer the other to our own self, when we accept his differences and his inviolable liberty. To accept the fact that some entity other than ours abides in him, not to pretend to answer all of his needs or to meet all of his expectations, is not to yield to infidelity. It is rather the ultimate proof of love, to want the other to remain faithful to his own self. It might mean some suffering for us, yet it is a fecund suffering that makes us forget about ourselves and live intensely that enriching possession. In the most amorous embrace, we embrace a free being, with all his potentials, some facets of which are still elusive to us.

To love is to welcome in the other whatever arouses our animal jealousy, sign of self-love and not of love. Love is communication, full of risks perhaps, but after the initial crisis, it begets a double growth.

There is nothing so deep as the sharing of each other's true personality. The other summons us, taking the chance of hurting us. The blow might crush us, yet, it forces us to let go of our possessive clasp in order that we become an other, a different person through the revelation of the other.

A love which is not a continued creation of one by the other, even at the cost of tragic tears, is the opposite of true love. To be worthy of love we must conquer it through a daily struggle against those sterilizing latent jealousies, in the painful burns of sex, in the absence, in the wounds of tenderness, in the doubt as to the ultimate significance of our engagement.

God's Eighth Day

Child, who art thou? Child. I mean the child. The child totally child: he who has to be taught everything; he who breaks a dish and blames it on the kitten; he who disturbs the still of night by his laughter; he who sees a ladybug as the eighth marvel of the world.

He who doesn't do anything of importance with his ten fingers; he who sometimes shakes his rattle. . . .

The child, of white linen and candor clad, who hates to

wash his hands, who steps into the puddles and often even stinks. . . .

He who takes everything and doesn't give it back. He who can say: "Draw me a sheep," but forgets to say "Thank you" once he has his sheep. . . .

He who believes, unaware that he is making an act of faith. . . .

He who hopes and loves simply because hope and love are part of his nature. . . .

He who would defy anything in the world, yet who is sure to be forgiven. . . .

He who stares at the flies during mass and who has tears in his eyes when he receives communion. . . .
He, the child!

And . . .
. . . what if the child was the last refuge to that despaired world of ours? What if child was the last word left as a rhyme to sacred?

. . . what if the child was God's eighth day? That point of convergence of a creation still howling, panting, in the pains of labor?

. . . what if the child was God's signature, the master's signature, in the right corner, at the bottom of his work?

so what?
. . . I can hear God laughing up there!
Well, listen, when you are surrounded by eternity, indeed, you can afford a good, an excellent joke . . .

A CHILD!

Respect of Our Neighbor

WE SHOULD NOT take others for granted. We must take a constant and faithful effort to go to others and give them our confidence. But what justifies that confidence? Nothing other than confidence itself. It is hardly necessary to justify it. Greatness is at the core of that "in spite of everything" feeling which we call respect. Or more simply: faith in life. If we persevere, in spite of the usual disappointments, and accept the other person, then something starts to grow in us. Suddenly, a new promise is revealed. Through us, the world becomes aware that it is alive, beautiful, and worthy of approval. A human being is only happy if we consider him capable of bringing happiness and if we let him know that he makes us happy. To make another happy by seeing his existence as part of our own happiness is respect through self-denial.

We honor the stranger by welcoming him in a disinterested way. It is only possible through a silent and intense act of perseverance in the way we accept the existence of the other. We should not expect others to acknowledge that we exist, or to come to us, but we should worry first about them, and then for them. We feel responsible for them. That silent acceptance, that positive worry, makes our world a little brighter, a little shinier.

The man who so behaves is quite vulnerable, but strength springs from his weakness. Self-denial helps him to welcome destiny, to bear no judgment, or to bring no condemnation. He welcomes totally the other's destiny. His behavior is not tainted with personal pretense nor any self-affirmation or search for his own sensitivity. As he acknowledges his neighbor's total self, his self-denial becomes a comforting and invigorating strength. He does not flee the present to aim at the impossible, at utopia. He simply tries to think for the other, to weigh, to evaluate the situation, to prepare the way.

It is awesome to see how life blooms when we see it with confidence. How men can change if we know how to judge them as superior to what they are and to treat them likewise, or if through a quiet, discreet respect, we assure them that they bear something good, beautiful and kind, something which lives in them, the bud of a promise. The lack of hope for greatness is the end of human existence, the destruction of life itself.

Your Brother Wants You!

To PRAY, first become aware of your brothers. Welcome them. Be silent in front of them. Listen to them in depth, perceiving beyond their words their hidden suffering or joy. Let those penetrate deep into your heart. Be self-effaced: give up your life for your brothers. Yes, your brothers must live in you, a presence fully alive, active, and warm. In your prayer, you will gather the voices of all men and make them raise to God.

The same applies to your faraway brothers. Don't scan the paper like a tourist, don't watch T.V. like an outsider, but try to be in communion with the real life of those men of which you receive the outside echoes through the media, for only then will your prayer become rich of all the life of the world.

At first, your prayer will be a plea for those who suffer spiritually and materially. You will understand what they miss the most, not so much the means to live as reasons to live. They are mostly longing for the light and the life of God. Intercede, beg our Father to grant them his light and his life, that they might treasure them in the bottom of their hearts.

Once you have seen in its depth the suffering of your brothers, you won't be satisfied to just pray for them. To make your prayer a true prayer you will have to commit your whole self to serve them.

A Space in The Sun

Have a happy day, my friend!
　　Take time to be happy,
　　You are a walking miracle!
　　On this earth, you are alone, unique,
　　One of a kind,
　　know that?

So, why aren't you astounded,
　　why aren't you happy,
　　why aren't you amazed,
　　at yourself and those around you?

Do you find it just normal,
　　just plain ordinary,
　　to be alive,
　　to breathe,
　　to sing, to dance,
　　to be happy?

So, why do you waste your time
　　in that mad race
　　after money and wordly goods?

　　In fact, my friend,
　　why do you worry so much
　　about tomorrow or after tomorrow?

　　Why do you quarrel?

　　Why are you bored?

　　Why do you indulge in foolish pleasure
　　and sleep when the sun shines?

Take time, quietly, softly,
time to be happy. . . .

Time is no expressway from crib to grave,

Time is a space,
    for you,
        to grow
            in the sun!

Joy in Our Brothers

TRUE JOY does not abide in the naive exaltation of a being out of touch with the world. Nor is it an "inner emigration." It is quite the opposite. It is by self-effacement and by reaching to our brother that we experience joy. Only the gift of our self can give courage to face reality, warmth toward other beings and that soft glow over everything which we call joy. The way to joy goes through self-denial. It is an undertaking which affects our whole existence. We must overthrow and demolish some of our selfishness, our laziness, our moodiness. In trying to shake the bonds of our pettiness, we can find a strength, a vitality hidden within ourselves. We discover it lying inside of us, like the cinders of a fire or like embers smothered long ago, that a simple draft can rekindle.

In a way, it is the same when we open up ourselves to our brother. The least thing that we do to him is a prerequisite condition to our own joy.

St. Luke tells us that on Ascension day, after Christ

was taken away from their sight, the disciples returned to Jerusalem with great joy. A strange joy! The face of the Lord is taken away from their sight and senses and with it goes the immediate experience of its glory. Yet, the heart of the disciples had already known joy when, on the first day of Easter week, they had been touched by the mysterious light of glory shining from the face of Christ. The event of Easter had created for them a new kind of closeness to the Lord, a visible one; one also felt by inner senses. Then Jesus' face was shining with the glow of the deep reconciliation and compassion. A glow, brighter than the sun, more dazzling than snow. In their hearts, the disciples were transformed. An inexpressible feeling had overcome them enkindling their hearts.

But, on Ascension day, another far more important change had taken place. Precisely because of Christ's departure, the joy of the disciples finds its fulfillment. It reaches a new state of perfection and maturity. That is why they returned, filled with great joy to their small world. When he was totally taken away from their senses, the Lord was freed from the narrow boundaries of human representation and even of any possibility of representation. He was entering a state of perfection that no eye has ever seen, of which no ear has ever heard, which has never been felt by the heart of any man. Contrary to their natural and human tendency, the disciples had suddenly realized that, from now on, they should look for joy in the invisible, beyond the visible, and that consequently, they could find joy everywhere because Christ is present everywhere. Therefore, we should not stare at the sky with wonderment, we must tend to worldly matters. Thus, our brother becomes the focus of our joy. The disciples also started to feel that the invisible and the inexpressible abide in the visible.

Exultet!

WHERE does music get that strange power? From the first measures, a spell is cast. Our hand so uptight, starts to loosen up, our breathing calms down, becoming deeper. In tune with the tempo of the symphony. I feel the pulsation of a new rhythm arising in me. A light, lingering breeze sweeps away worries, annoyances, anxieties. Here I am, singing, dancing in a land where Mozart entices me. Whatever gives spice to life, risk, tragedy, splendor even is present yet dons that bounce, that playfulness, that gracefulness in which appears an ultimate form of life. Amazement, exultation, gratitude!

There is some of that inner dance in the celebration of our faith. We have not fully expressed it as long as we have not let ourselves be enraptured by the jubilation of music. A state of song. An allegro.

Certain aspects of our universe already set us on the road of such gratuitous prodigality. The whole world, in its inexhaustible splendor is offered to man. Only the destruction of his natural environment or the corruption of his senses could prevent him from marveling at the universe. What a sight! And graciously offered! Why the extravagant shapes and colors of some flowers, of some birds or of the submarine flora? As if one secret of life was profusion, excess gratuity.

The mere experience of action teaches us gratitude. As necessary as it might be, the effort alone is rarely sufficient for the successful outcome of the act. Last minute maturity, outstanding achievements come unexpectedly, without warning, freely. The artisan, the man of action, the artist are well aware that their success is not the fruit of their work, but that it has been bestowed upon them and, most

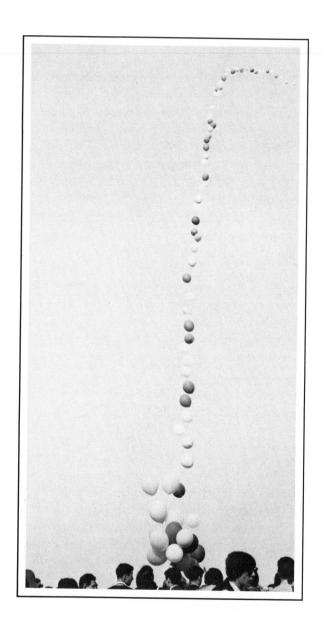

of the time, quite by surprise.

However, it is in the realm of people that we truly see the abundance of the futile. Gratuity is the luxury, the daily bread which each one of us needs to become himself. That is why it is necessary to evaluate any investment according to a criterion of efficiency and also to proceed to a distribution of riches according to a strict justice. And then, what could become of a world ruled by efficiency alone? Supposing that everybody felt that it is the way to go, how many are there who dare to advocate a politic of gift economics? Oh! May time come for love! Love has its reasons but it reveals its true essence beyond any motivations, as it goes on giving itself, unconditionally, unaltered. Since natural life is profusion, excess, folly, how could love be parsimonious, thrift minded, reasonable?

Yes, at the heart of our faith, of its celebration, we do proclaim an absolute folly!

The beauty of our world, the song of our liberty, the splendor of our love, everything is given to us. Free, graciously. A gift to us also is our encounter with the gospel and the horizons it opened for us. Gracious was the gift, gratuitous the response. So, how not to give thanks?

Presence? Absence?

NOTHING can replace the presence of a beloved one. There is no use even trying. We must bear that in mind and hold fast. What seems so hard can become of great comfort, since this unfilled emptiness is still a bond. It is wrong to say that God will fill that void. On the contrary, as painful as it might sound, he purposely maintains it in order to help us keep our old bonds of communion. The more beautiful and rich our memories, the harder it is to take the separation. However, gratefulness turns the pain of memories into a sweet joy. We carry within ourselves the beauty of the past, not as a thorn, but as a precious gift. We should refrain from reverting too often to our memories, or even from relying upon them. A precious gift is like a hidden treasure. A treasure which is ours, we know it, and yet we can just admire it at a few given moments. Only then will a lasting joy, a steadfast strength spring out of the past. Furthermore, time of separation is not wasted time or sterile time for our common life, at least it does not need to be. On the contrary, in spite of all the problems that it brings, separation can help weave amazingly strong bonds of communion.

Come and Sit by Me

"COME AND SIT by me on the bench, in front of the house, wife. After all, you have some right to it! Soon we'll have been together for forty years.

Tonight, since it is such a nice evening and also the twilight of our lives, you deserve a little rest, you see.

Here we are. Our children are on their own, launched in the world and we are alone again, like at first.

Wife, do you remember? We started from nothing. Everything was left for us to do. We tried our hardest. It was tough! One needs courage, perseverance.

One needs love too and love is not what we think it is at first.

It is more than kisses, sweet words whispered in the ear, or closeness to each other. Life is a long time, the wedding day comes just once. It is well after, remember, that we really started in life.

In life what one does is undone, it must be redone and is undone again.

The children come. They have to be fed, clothed, raised. It never ends. Sometimes they are sick. You were up all night and I had to work from morning till night.

Sometimes we lose hope. The years go by and it seems that we are at a standstill, that we even go backwards.

You do remember, wife, don't you?

All those worries, all those anxieties. But you were there. We stayed faithful to each other, I was able to lean upon you and you upon me.

We were fortunate to be together. Both were set to do the job, we lasted, we held fast.

True love is not what one thinks it is. True love is not a one day affair, it is an everyday commitment.

Then, as the days go by, everything works out for the best. The children have turned out as fine kids, we had set the example.

We have consolidated the foundations of the house: may all the houses in this country be sturdy and so will our country be.

So, please, now sit close to me, and then, look, for time has come for harvest and for storing the crop.

The dusk is pink, and a pink haze arises among the trees.

Come close to me. Let's not even talk. We do not need to say anything. We only need to be together once more and to let night fall over the satisfaction of the well accomplished task."

-------••⟨∞⟩••-------

That I May Cry!

HAPPY is he who has found the humane grace of tears. Jesus cried over Jerusalem, over Lazarus, and, may be, out of tenderness over Mary Magdalene. Inner dryness leaves us parched, like soil deprived of rain. Soap opera actors have given to sobs the stigma of melodrama, yet they are the ultimate sign of the tragic conscience.

Between the cry of the child as he enters a life he does not understand and the cry of the adult over a death he cannot understand lies our mystery.

The moment he pierced that mystery, Pascal cried out of joy. . . .

-------••⟨∞⟩••-------

Tenderness Above All

GOD's tenderness is oblivious to our human self-regard. It rests in the hearts of the tenderness of men, the way they are. We find proof of that in a quite peculiar detail. The risen Christ first appears to the ones who have known how to love him with their hearts. Women. Yes. Isn't it strange to find that the risen Christ doesn't appear first to the apostles but to Mary Magdalene and her companions, who, prophetesses of love, will go and tell the news to the disciples. It doesn't mean that men do not know how to love with their heart or that tenderness is weakness, a woman's trait. If women seem to have a greater need for tenderness, isn't it because they know better than men how to give it?

Tenderness is love that knows how to give, love that knows how to receive: a wonderful exchange?

Tenderness will not let itself be confined by a definition. If you were asked to define a summer morning's breeze, what would you answer? A quiver? A caress? As you can see, this is not a definition. Asked to talk about the unaffected beauty of islands, unaware that they are queens of the earth and of the sea, what would you answer? And what about the feather-light steps of the mother and father entering their child's room? That is tenderness. That respect, born of love, for those things we just dare touch with our eyes, that is tenderness. Tenderness lies at the core of love, as poetry is at the core of things. Love's sweetness, limpidity, finesse. It is not an extrinsic or superimposed quality, it is love.

So, please grant yourself an alm of tenderness. Just two pennies' worth of tenderness in your relationship with others and you will discover that even faithfulness to the commandments, which might seem so cold, is not plain conformity to a law by which we must abide but the blossoming of a liberty of the heart which brings out the true attitude of love.

Just two pennies' worth of tenderness in your relationship with God and you will discover that faith is a dialogue of love: "He who loves me, I will love him and I shall manifest myself to him." It is real declaration of love that God makes to each one of us. He says: "I love you." Isn't it marvelous that God himself doesn't want to say more than man would say when he cannot find any more to say? When one says: "I love you" from the bottom of the heart, those words get stuck in one's throat. Tenderness is a whisper.

Even better: it is love's silent desire.

Finally, add one ounce of tenderness to your prayer and if you happen to think that you don't know how to pray anymore, that you do not enjoy praying, you will find that with just a little tenderness you can pray as you would hum a song, all day long, a song you love but the words of which you don't know too well and a song that you kind of transpose in major, in minor, according to the day or even the hours of the day.

Tenderness is love's genius, always improvising. It bestows upon silences between people the full weight of intuitive communication.

It gives to words between people the perfect inflection of love's dialogue.

It imparts to plain gestures between people the intelligence of newness.

Let us live in that intelligence of love. Let us live that experience of love. It could well be that God may sing in our heart: "Don't tell me too much about love... but, please, from time to time, tell me some tender words!"

Visage

Faraway closeness...
    Visage.
A simple spring
    concealed.

Endless, wandering quest...
    Visage,
remembered for the tenderness of a glance.
Pearl nestled in the folds of our nights.

Visage of Jesus, humane visage of God.
"He who sees me, sees the Father" (John: 14,9)
Jesus, visage of the Father.

A child, so very near to his mother:
    God present to our world.
Visage, unique visage, for us to contemplate love.

Silence, respectful presence,
may that visage "the eyes of our heart enlighten"
(Eph. 1:18)
Visage of the child, visage of God,
    to contemplate
by the light of the gospel,
    in the secret of our selves.

Visage,
    revelation of God's fidelity
and of his faithful compassion.

I

Time and Times

Lord, I have time,
I have all my time,
all the time you give to me,
the years of my life,
the days of my years,
the hours of my days,
they belong to me.
It is up to me to fill them, quietly, calmly,
but to fill them completely, to the end,
to offer them to you, so that with their insipid water
you make a generous wine, like of yore in Cana,
for a human wedding.
Lord, I do not even ask you for time to do this,
and then that,
I just ask you for the grace to do conscientiously
what you want me to do, in the time you grant me.

Serenity

SLOGANS and ads should promise peace and silence. Anyone who wants to escape is in search of those, at least
confusedly. He wants to forget noise and agitation.

We must not make our vacation time a time of super-
excitement, of super-rhythm, of superficial life, but a more
intense time of life, by being calmer, by allowing all those
wordly things to satiate our soul instead of leaving it dried
out.

Consider the wonders of the world. They tell of God's greatness to the one who asks them and who knows how to wait in silence for their answer. There are the accomplishments of science, wealth, art, and sport. They tell of man's power. Yet, to the one who asks and knows how to listen to their answer in silence, they teach not to be proud of heart, not to be haughty, not to be arrogant, for the greatness of man is to live as a child of God, in collaboration with his Father. If, with our eyes wide open, we experience the great things of this world, the greatness of man with God, if in silence, eyes closed, we experience the peace God grants to those who work with him, then can we, in the middle of a world sometimes hard to bear, of a world in despair, find hope again, in the whole of mankind. Mankind is rightly proud of what it does, because it does it with God.

Like Joan of Arc in Paul Claudel's oratorio: this little girl, humble and proud at the same time, whose dialogue with Brother Dominic goes like this:

I am the one who did it!

It is God! God is the one who did it!

It is God, God who did it with Joan!

And ourselves, why could not a dialogue like this with the Lord start each day of our vacation?

"Anyone who wishes to be first, will be the last of all and the servant of all . . . whoever receives one such little child for my sake, receives me; and whoever receives me, receives not me but him who sent me." (Mark 9:35)

"Lord, my heart is not proud,

Nor haughty my eyes;

I busy myself not with great things,

Nor with things too deep for me.

For my soul I keep
In peace and silence.
Like a child against his mother's breast,
So is my soul in peace with me.
O Israel, hope in the Lord,
Now and forever!
O Lord, Master of life,
Thank you for those familiar things:
Bread, wind, earth, water;
For those simple men
In whom all is light,
For music and silence,
For rhythm and rest;
Thank you for the peace
That comes from you;
Thank you for being so close to us
Through your child, Jesus Christ.

My Destiny Is In Your Hands

MY DESTINY... it is I. I who have lived, who lives and still
would love to live a little bit longer. It is that self of mine
with all that I understand and all that I do not understand.
With what I can do and what I cannot do. With my strong
points and my weaknesses, with my good qualities as well as
my defects. My destiny... it is I—with that generous voca-
tion to love God, my Lord, with all my heart, with all my
mind, with all my strength and also to love my neighbor as
myself. My destiny... it is I, with that abyss of lies and

perversion that I bear in me. Lord, the way I was, am now and ever shall be, the way you know me, my true self. Yes, Lord, in your hands, I am.

My destiny is in your hands. When something is in someone's hands, it usually belongs to him, at least for the moment. We assume that he needs it, uses it and, therefore, takes care of it. I am not talking about the hands of just any man, Lord, but of your hands. The hands of God. If my destiny is in your hands, Lord, it is because it is yours from the beginning and till the end. Forever for you to use. Therefore, you will take care of it, as you will take care of me, without any limits, for ever and ever.

My destiny is not in my own hands. How truly happy I am not to have to rely upon myself as an authority whose wisdom I must honor and admire, but also question and whose silly mistakes would frighten me at every moment. How good it feels not to be my own master, not to have my destiny in my hands alone. That my destiny, the story of my life, myself, all of these rest in the hands of God.

You might ask: "But does God have hands?" Indeed he does! Quite different from our claws. Much more deft and strong. You might also wonder: "What do we really mean by 'the hands of God'?" Let us put it this way: the hands of God are his acts, his works, his words. They surround us. They contain us. They carry us, they keep us. We could say or even see this as an image or as a symbol, but here is a point beyond image and symbol. A point where the hands of God have to be taken literally and seriously. A point where the acts, the works and the divine words have their beginning, their center, their end. Your hands. The hands of our Savior, Jesus Christ. Those hands he stretched out when he called and said: "Come to me, all you who labor and are burdened, and I will give you rest." (Matt. 11:28). Those hands that blessed the children. Those hands that touched and healed the sick. Those hands that broke and distributed the bread to the five thousand in the desert and to the disciples before his death. Finally, but most important, those hands that were nailed to the cross for our reconciliation with God. Yes, those hands are the hands of God! Those strong, fatherly hands, good, gentle, and tender. Those hands, friendly, faithful, merciful, and kind. Those divine hands in which our destiny rests. Those hands in which we are ourselves.

That Twinkle In God's Eye

YOU CARRY within you the secret desire to live in constant prayer. You feel that life in the presence of God is the source of all joy, of all peace, of all real happiness. Yet, if you would add up those minutes, those hours you waste in your day, you would have plenty of time to pray.

From time to time, set five minutes aside for a break and try to make inner silence. Your only preoccupation should be to stay, silent and quiet, in the presence of your living God. Along your days, don't let an hour go by without taking a quick inner dive to the bottom of your heart in the presence of the Most High. Remember how often you can call to God for help, for love, for gratitude, even if it is just a breath long plea.

To live in constant prayer, learn how to welcome the present moment. Take it as a gift of God. Your life itself will become a prayer the day you entrust your whole being

to the Father, in the sacrifice of Jesus. Your existence will become a spiritual offering to the glory of the Trinity. Yet, that offering, that gift of yourself becomes true and real only when you let God lead you to the shores he has chosen for you. Indeed, you would like to choose your own offering but God is asking for something else, probably for what you hold as the dearest. Let God choose in your life whatever pleases him: this will become your spiritual sacrifice. Then you will be totally receptive to the action of God in you.

The present moment is the only time in your life when you can become one with him, in his essential being. You have no power over the past for it belongs to his mercy, you have no idea of the future for it is entrusted in his providence; so, the only moment left to you is the present one, open window over eternity. The twinkle of God's eye: the only moment in which you can reach him.

He who has the present moment has God,

And whoever has the present moment has everything.

The present moment is enough,

May nothing trouble you.

Be Frugal With Time

BE FRUGAL with time, and time will belong to you. You do not own time beforehand, nor must it own you. Yes, receive and welcome the forthcoming time as a gift. Time is given to you, with its newness of each day, which you cannot recognize if you foresee too much.

Be kind to time. Once it has been given to you, take it. But please, do not mistreat it, do not force it, do not try to fill it up with more than it can hold. Time comes day by day. Each day holds the heritage of the day just past, and you are its heir.

Sometimes you might cry over wasted or misused time, but what is the taste of your tears? If it is of frustration, who will be of solace to you? You are drowning yourself, you wallow in your tears. If it is over your sins that you cry, remember that they are washed away by your tears. When the sun shines after the rain, doesn't everything seem more beautiful?

When times are hard, forgive the bad weather. Hold fast! Do not change decisions already made, yet do not make more decisions seeking escape through activism. Time's forgiveness is holy patience. As if God would ask for your forgiveness when you are suffering and cannot understand the purpose of that pain. For a day of patience, God will forgive much lost time.

But remember that time is not to be wasted. You must earn your bread. Time is not just money. Not to waste your time will often mean lavishing it on others or giving it up for justice's sake; then be sure that you won't get bored! When evening comes on those well-filled days, those days enriched with what you have given, you will be fully satisfied.

Have a pure heart and a simple intention in regard to time. Do not try too hard to organize your time, such as which hours you will give to God, which you will give to others, and which you will keep for yourself. Let yourself see God in time, not only in time of prayer, but in that of work, of leisure, of love.

Your time, so scattered, so whimsical, so frustrated, your time crammed with contradictions, may also be a time of peace. It can be a time of peace if you are not its slave; in spite of schedules and routines of life, which are real, whether we acknowledge them or not. Nothing is less peaceful than today's time. That is why every morning when you receive it, every evening when you gather it, it will be even more necessary for you to think of the one who gave it to you, as a father to his child.

A Time For Everything

WE MUST find God and love him through what he gives us at the present time. If it pleases him to grant us an amazing happiness on this earth, let us not be more devout than he is! Let us not spoil our happiness with some provocative thoughts or an overzealously religious imagination, because we simply cannot be satisfied with what he gives us. God will see that he who finds him through happiness in this world and gives him grace for it, has many a time to be reminded that, on earth, all is temporary and that it is a good idea to familiarize our hearts with eternity. There will be times when we might say quite sincerely: "Oh, how I would love to be up there!" Yet, there is a time for everything. The essential is to adjust our steps to God's steps, not to be a few lengths ahead, yet not to stay behind him either. How foolish to want all at once, marital happiness, a cross to carry, and even a foretaste of the celestial Jerusalem, where there is no man or woman as such. For there is a time for everything. "A time to weep, a time to laugh . . . a time to embrace and a time to refrain from embracing, a time to mend and a time to sew . . . God will seek time that has been driven away." (Eccl. 3)

This last verse means, I think, that nothing of our past is ever lost, that God will seek again with us what has been driven away but is still part of ourselves. When the nostalgia of time gone by overcomes us, usually at the oddest times, may we see it as one of those numerous hours God keeps in store for us, and may we remember that he forbids us to relive the past on our own, without his help.

Kindness

THE ESSENCE of Christian kindness is not some abstract affirmation or a set attitude to face reality. It is the person of Jesus Christ. Only through the silent contemplation of Christ's kindness can we acquire that spirit of kindness to which we are called as Christians. The longer we contemplate the face of Christ, the more we are penetrated by the plenitude of his mysterious presence. In our daily contact with his person and his feelings, appears his really amazing kindness. His goodness shows a perfect inner freedom, a complete peace of soul. Christ, as a man, was so fully aware that he did not need opposition or hostility to be enkindled as we usually do. In this world torn by hate, the total absence of hostility had finally been realized, in Christ.

Christ's kindness was his receptiveness. A receptiveness that would beget truth where there was confusion. Kindness generates an extraordinary plenitude of truth. Through kindness man is able, in the most insignificant events of his life, as well as in the least of his encounters, to awaken the existential truth which lies asleep in other men. Truth, on a backdrop of kindness is tactful. Blunt honesty hurts, for it reflects only a few facets of the truth and comes out of a somewhat hostile ground. The powerful kindness of Christ, untainted by hostility, fully receptive, was dictated by an almost motherly concern for any human being. It was also a disposition to offer shelter to the striving existence of others. It was the attitude of someone who had chosen not to make any creature suffer.

In Love With Life

THERE IS, in the most beautiful part of Tiergarten, a splendid poplar which I see every day. Straight, proud but not arrogant, it whispers and quivers with life. I have named it the tree of life.

By looking at it, by touching it, I confronted a sad reality: who has ever taught us how to use the resources of our imagination or, rather, to explore its truth and depth? Who has ever taught us to look at a tree, to touch it while we let grow, bring to life, resurrect in ourselves that backdrop of images, archetypes that we carry within us, like those roots, source of life, its noble carriage, its strength, the swaying of its foliage. We are mutilated. We have been deprived of that experience under pretense of rationality. Our imagination has been confined to a mental asylum. No wonder that it has become crazy, for it has been severed from life and truth. It lies, at the bottom of ourselves, screeching with pain, thirst, despair. Thus, it gives birth to monsters.

Could we be our own enemy? I believe that we can slowly become just that. I believe that there is somewhere a place, a field, maybe a little space in this world where we do become our own enemy, but I also believe that there is a place, a field, a space where we can slowly make peace with our own self. How can we enter it? Maybe by merely trying to find it, by the pure act of searching, not too sure of the object of our quest but firmly decided to look for everything, ask for everything.

To A Rose

ONCE, there was a prince who owned a magnificent diamond, which was his pride and joy. One day, an accident happened and the precious gem was badly scratched. The prince sent for the finest craftsmen to restore the jewel's beauty. In spite of all their efforts, they could not remove the scratch. Finally, there came a jeweler of unsurpassed talent. With art, and with patience he etched a magnificent rose into the diamond and skillfully turned the scratch into the stem of the rose, so that the gem appeared more beautiful than ever before.

Isn't this precisely what Christ has done with our human condition? He has accepted our nature, with all its dimensions, its wounds, its hardships: thus we have no right to the hardships we meet as if they were limitations and worries, for they bear a new meaning. We are aware of the narrow boundaries of our language, of our ordinary life and its routine, yet, let us not forget that we betray their real meaning by not looking beyond those shortcomings. Through the sacraments Christ invites us to nourish this hope. Our weakness, our weariness, our relationships to others are no longer a hell. We have come out of the darkness. It is up to us to transform our scratches into the stem of a rose!

Please, Anything But That!

"AND, JESUS, looking straight at him, loved him." One of the most moving sentences of the gospel. What happened in that look? That man, how was he looking at God while God was looking straight at him? The eyes of God meeting the eyes of man. The gospel does not say: "Jesus, because he loved him, looked straight at him." It shows a certain progression—Jesus looked straight at him, then loved him. Because Christ has taken time to love, to scrutinize, he finds that he loves him, even more than he thought. Not only does Jesus respect his quest but he, himself, acknowledges it by going beyond. In love, Jesus has also gone beyond by taking time to love. Faith is not a unilateral progression. God walks with us. It is as if we had something quite difficult to say and Christ would "break the ice" all at once and say: "You really mean it, don't you? Well, in that case, listen, here is what I have to tell you... I wouldn't have said it if you had not asked for it. Yes, there is just one thing lacking: go, sell whatever you have and give it to the poor, then you will have a treasure in heaven. Come, follow me!"

Just one thing lacking. Not some optional thing, not one of those superfluous things. Not a degree of perfection which could be acquired on top of everything else. The very heart of things: the cross. The exigence of poverty that Christ presents to the rich man, touches him in what is the dearest to him, not so much in what he is as in what he has. Christ means, "Do not be a failure to your own self," and the young man replies the way we would reply: "Oh! please, no! Anything but that!" We play on God the trick he played on us in the Garden of Eden! We each have an untouchable tree and we admonish God: "If you ever touch it, we are no longer masters of our destiny!" Scandalous as it may sound, God does not respect private property! We could hang signs like "beware of dog" or "no trespassing" along the fence of our little parcel of life, yet Christ would jump over those and tell us: "Leave everything." Such is God's audacity! He calls us to sanctity. To be a saint is to plant our tree in a soil other than our carefully selected Garden of Eden. We must transplant it, prune it, and realize that it is no more than stump. Like the tree planted before spring time. No branches, just two arms.

The cross is a tree, a maimed tree. The cross always provokes the core of our being. To the rich young man, his cross is poverty. To another, it is something else. The authenticity of our search for God is tested in our attitude toward questions that faith asks us in a theoretical manner, but in accepting God's intervention in our life. The young rich man is a nice, earnest fellow. He does not try to justify his own incapacity to say yes, by comparing it to the incapacity of others. He doesn't excuse himself by blaming his mediocrity upon the institutions of the church or some intellectual objections.

When Christ tells him: "You will have a treasure in heaven," he does not mean a compensation or a deal. Christ places the cross in the very dimension of the resurrection. He tells him, "In the way you choose to live and see beyond the loss that such poverty means to you, will you discover the real treasure. At those words a cloud of darkness surrounded the young man. His face fell. He went away, wrapped up in his own sadness, the sadness of the impossible. Yes, he had great wealth, says the gospel. . . ."

Forceful Call

BOUNDLESS LOVE is an intruder. Maybe I've had kind of a passive coexistence with God. Maybe I've believed that I was more or less O.K. as far as my soul was concerned, feeling more or less at peace. Maybe I dreamed of a peaceful, happy twilight to my life.

And, suddenly, all those visions are shattered by some divine summons. God asks from me the unexpected. It is like the announcement of an unwanted child.

Should I lend an ear to that call? Should I take such a hard decision? Why, really? Everything was going so smoothly! Do I need those uncertainties, those new anxieties? Must I live again through the stumbles of the first call, how long past? Must I leave my familiar country, not knowing where God will lead me?

I have not told God those things, but nevertheless I have felt them. Of course, it was not a flat "no" to the Lord, but kind of a polite refusal, like: "Oh, please let the man I am still live before you!"

The man I am . . . that man, who represents an actual condition, a well-defined situation, a conjuncture of things in which he is set, maybe a relationship with God which seems good enough to him. What else could he wish?

Boundless love is an intruder into my life. It jolts my existence. It comes to break what appears to be stable. It also comes to open new horizons of which I was unaware.

Shall I refuse? Shall I flee away from the call to me? If I refuse, shall I become a stranger to love, to any kind of love? The love for which I shall settle then will also be quite relative and limited. It will be the rejection of Absolute Love, of its challenge. Still waters instead of the deep sea.

Lord of Love, free me from my moorings! I shall not sail back to you, shores so familiar. May the one I shall become, O Lord of Love, live in your eyes!

An Art of Dying, An Art of Living

THE ART of dying must be applied to our whole life. Joyful, open, gleeful, wholesome is the life of the man, who, day by day, prepares himself to die and lives ready for his own death. The old wise men, men of faith, know what that age-old saying expressed: "He who does not die before his death will know a real death when death comes to him." And Goethe echoes in his well known quatrain: "As long as you have not made dying and becoming a part of yourself, just a somber stranger on a somber earth will you be." And those lines, familiar to us, thanks to the poetry of Angelus Silesius: "Christ could have been born a thousand times, if he is not born in you, you would still be lost."

All is grace when one receives it as grace. We must let ourselves be grasped, that is the whole thing. To let ourselves be grasped by the whole reality, without ever refusing its harshness, its cruelty, its conflicts. Upon that cruel backdrop, to live the sweetness of God, of men, to live the dialogue of the visible and of the invisible, of time and of eternity. For that we must have learned and experienced love in our life.

Actually, the art of dying is another opportunity to love. It is an art pertaining to the divine art through which God became man so that man would become God. To die with serenity to ourself everyday; to accept with lucidity endless deceptions, to accept with lucidity that small and big vanities, follies, weaknesses fade away, to accept with lucidity being cheated, used, offended; to accept threats, injustices, words of hate, mockery. Yes, to accept to die, little by little, each day, means, even if we do it with serenity, that we must become the source which flows and overflows joyfully, without ever wondering how its water will be used. It means that we must become the tree in full bloom, breeze-swept by the breath of God and of the world, which loses its foliage in the fall but still is not bitten by the harsh winter frost. It means that we must also become the field, laden with seed, yet serenely bearing the weight of the snow, in the hope and in the certainty of the resurrection when springtime comes.

Death

ETERNITY does not exist in another life. Not even in another world. Not even outside of time.

Eternity exists in this life, in this world which is the only world, in our human history which is the only history.

Yes, there is a realm which is inaccessible to death. A realm that exists nowhere else than in a life which is fully human, that is divine, and conscious of participating in creation.

To meditate upon death is to meditate upon life, upon its deep reality, upon its meaning.

My life bears dimensions of eternity, not for after this

life, not beyond it, but here and now, as I am a workman in charge of a project well above my capacities.

My life bears dimensions of eternity, not for after this life, not beyond it, but here and now as I have the certainty that love in its ultimate form cannot be fulfilled in a you to me perspective but in one which unfolds from me to everything through the other.

Love alone can save us from death.

Because, finally, what is death if not simply a tremendous love? It is the gift of our uniqueness to the other and through him to the whole creation. Saint Teresa of Avila perceived it marvelously well by foreseeing in death the sublime communion with the eternal lover.

Yes, my life bears dimensions of eternity, not for after this life,

not beyond this life,

but now,

as I am conscious of participating in the continued act of creation.

In Te Domine Speravi

ONE MORE WORD about death and the feelings I would like to have at that moment: to think I shall discover tenderness. One sure thing, God won't deceive me. Such a conjecture is aberrant. I shall go to him and I shall tell him: "Lord, I do not avail myself of anything, except of my trust in your goodness." In that trust lies my strength, my only strength. If the trust and confidence I have in your love would abandon me, my whole self would be shattered. If happiness belongs only to the few who are worthy of it, I'd better forget about it!

Yet, the more I go, the more I see my Father as infinite goodness. Our spiritual masters can profess whatever they fancy, argue about justice, fear, exigence, why should I care? My judge, my only judge is the one who, every day used to go up the watchtower scanning the horizon for a prodigal son who might be on his way home. So, tell me, who wouldn't love to appear in front of such a judge?

. . . O Father, thank you for your love!

Take Life As It Comes . . .

THE WAY of faith is the way of life. The way of every day of our life is the way of the forever. The life of forever. Not just a thing, but someone: the risen Christ! The famous words of Saint Paul: "For me, to live is Christ," echo the equally famous words of Jesus: "I am the way, the life." Let us notice the juxtaposition: Jesus does not say: "I am the way of life," he says: "the way, the life." The truth also, since the way has to be the right one. Way, life, truth: essentially identical.

To meet the risen Christ, it is not enough to be just on the way. To be on the way reflects a passive attitude. We are asked to take the way. To take it the right way. We are asked to take life as it comes. Life comes from Christ. Life goes to Christ. Life is the right way, Christ is the right guide. That is why the road to Emmaüs is typical of the itinerary of our Christian faith.

We stand at the threshold of the adventure of faith

which lies wide open before us. Our eyes must become familiar with the landscape, in order to understand the outline of the road, and to recognize the signs along the way. Why should we be afraid of wandering? A way along which one does not dare to take the time to pick up a simple weed is a joyless way. The essential is not so much to glean ideas about faith as it is to let Christ come to us the way he wants to come. Let us not scare the Spirit away with our animosity and our bitterness. Like the bird, only in the silence of a serene road does the Spirit let us approach him. May our hearts be filled with admiration, for Saint Paul's words, some twenty centuries old, are still true: "God grants us assurance of confident access to him through the way of faith." (Eph. 3:12). God himself reveals to us that faith is a challenge!

Beggar of Hope

Beggar of the day,
In my hands I take you,
as one in his hands takes
a lamp for the night,
and you become
the glare which dissipates darkness.

Beggar of the fire,
In my hands I take you
as one in his hands takes
a fire for the winter

and you become
the blaze that sweeps the world.

Beggar of hope,
In my hands I take you
as one in his hands takes
the source for the summer
and you become
torrent of eternal life.

Beggar of you
In my hands I take you
as in his hands one takes
the pearl of love;
and you become
the treasure for the joy of the prodigal.

Beggar of God
In my hands I take you
as in your hand you take
mine
for that day;
and I become
the one you sent
to the beggar of the earth

———◦∞◦———

Joy!

Joy is the sun
to those who long for its light,
Joy is the Lord to me,
For my sun he is.
Its light arouses me,
His shine my darkness dispels.

Eyes he gave me,
And the day of his glory I saw,
Ears he gave me,
And his truth I received,
Wisdom he gave me,
And in love with him I fell.

The path of deceit I rejected,
His serenity he gave me,
And his salvation to bring me back to him.
The gifts of his grace he bestowed upon me
And to his glory he created me.
For his name, white in my garb.
Transfigured I am.
For his goodness I turned away
From perishable things.

What is bound to die
Worthless is to my eyes.
By his word evil lies defeated.
Eternal life has flourished
In the land of the Lord,
As promised to the faithful
And granted to those who hope in him.

Acknowledgements

1. **Wind of Love**
   P. TALEC, *Les choses de la foi,* Ed. Centurion, 1973, p. 296

2. **To Pray Is Impossible**
   M. BELLET, "La place vide," *Christus,* oct. 1977, n° 96, pp. 404–405

3. **Patience ... Silence ...**
   B. ARMINJON, "Progresser," *Christus,* oct. 1970, n° 68, pp. 508

4. **At Night They Stood**
   M. de CERTEAU, "Expérience Spirituelle," *Christus,* oct. 1970, n° 68, pp. 489–490

5. **Silence and Word**
   L. BOROS, *Rencontrer Dieu dans l'homme,* Ed. Desclée, Ed. Paulines, 1971, pp. 158–159

6. **As I Listen to You**
   P. JACQUEMONT, J.P. JOSUA, B. QUELQUEJEU, *Une foi exposée,* Ed. Cerf, 1973, pp. 92–93

7. **Yes, I Do Know You**
   Un moine de l'Eglise d'Orient, *Amour sans limites,* Ed. Chevetogne, 1971, pp. 9–11

8. **Let There Be Light**
   Un moine de l'Eglise d'Orient, *Amour sans limites,* Ed. Chevetogne, 1971, pp. 34–35

9. **Quest of God ...**
   Y. RAGUIN, *Chemins de la contemplation,* Ed. Desclée de Brouwer, 1969, pp. 25–27

10. **When You Hide**
    P. LYONNET, *Prières pour le temps de la maladie,* Ed. Epi, 1965, pp. 27–29

11. **A Farewell to Ourselves**
    Y. RAGUIN, *Chemins de la contemplation,* Ed. Desclée de Brouwer, 1969, pp. 28–30

24. **Is It Ever Too Late?**

L. BOROS, *Rencontrer Dieu dans l'homme,* Ed. Desclée, Ed. Paulines, 1971, pp. 31–32

25. **Love**

R. GARAUDY, *Parole d'homme,* Ed. R. Laffont, 1975, pp. 43–45

26. **God's Eighth Day**

D. DECOIN, *Il fait Dieu,* Ed. Julliard, 1975, pp. 66–67

27. **Respect of Our Neighbor**

L. BOROS, *Rencontrer Dieu dans l'homme,* Ed. Desclée, Ed. Paulines, 1971, pp. 49–50

28. **Your Brother Wants You!**

J. LAFRANCE, *Prie ton Père dans le secret,* Abbaye Sainte Scholastique, Dourgne, 1977, pp. 227–229

29. **A Space in The Sun**

P. BOSMANS, *Aimer,* Ed. Desclée, 1975, p. 9

30. **Joy in Our Brothers**

L. BOROS, *Rencontrer Dieu dans l'homme,* Ed. Desclée, Ed. Paulines, 1971, pp. 64–65

31. **Exultet!**

P. JACQUEMONT, J.P. JOSUA, B. QUELQUEJEU, *Une foi exposée,* Ed. Cerf, 1973, pp. 157–158

32. **Presence? Absence?**

D. BONHOEFFER, *Résistance et soumission,* Ed. Labor et Fides, Genève, 1967, pp. 87–88

33. **Come and Sit By Me ...**

A. RAMUS, *Livret de Mariage du Canton de Vaud* (Suisse)

34. **That I May Cry!**

M. SINNIGER, *Frany,* Ed. Centurion, 1974, p. 39

35. **Tenderness Above All**

P. TALEC, *Les choses de la foi,* Ed. Centurion, 1975, pp. 291–293

36. **Visage**

J.M. CAILLAUX, *Un sourire de Dieu,* Ed. Pneumathèque, 1975, pp. 23, 26–27

50. In Te Domine Speravi

A. VALENSIN, *La joie dans la foi,* Ed. Aubier-Montaigne, 1967, pp. 95–96

51. Take Life As It Comes...

P. TALEC, *Les choses de la foi,* Ed. Centurion, 1973, pp. 16–17

52. Beggar of Hope...

D. RIMAUD, *Les arbres dans la mer,* © C.N.P.L. Paris 1970. All rights reserved.

53. Joy!

Liturgie ambrosienne

Recontrer Dieu dans l'homme and *A nous l'avenir* by L. BOROS were published originally by Matthias-Grünewald-Verlag and are reprinted with permission. *Meeting God in Man* was published in English by Seabury Press and Search Press.

Prayers, by Michel Quoist, and *Faut-il encore pratiquer?* by Bernard Bro are copyright 1963 by Sheed & Ward.

Biographical Notes

Louis Christiaens is a native of the North of France. He was born in Lille in 1935 and was an officer in the French Air Force during the war in Algeria.

A law professor, he is presently teaching political science at the state university of Nancy, France, where he is also a counselor to students and director of a student center.

He has traveled extensively in foreign countries and has given many retreats in the U.S. and Canada. The editor of the monthly Jesuit magazine *Etudes,* he is the author of many works to raise consciousness about juridical and socio-political problems relating to abortion, drugs, suicide, socialized medicine, etc.

Quest for God represents some milestones on his itinerary as a pilgrim of life. . . .

Marie-Odile Fortier-Masek is the French born wife of an American citizen. She has spent the last 16 years in the U.S. where she taught languages at Boston University, in the Middle West and at Chapman College.

She has translated and adapted several books and is the author of a Spanish grammar.

Her main interest is raising seven active children. It is also in the spirit of a *Quest for God* that she and her husband have participated to this book, a joyful hymn to life and to their hope.